Bread Machine Baking for All Seasons

Connie Merydith

PRIMA PUBLISHING

© 1997 by Connie Merydith

PRIMA PUBLISHING and colophon are registered trademarks of Prima Communications, Inc.

Library of Congress Cataloging-in-Publication Data

Merydith, Connie.
   Bread machine baking for all seasons : delightful recipes for year-round pleasure / Connie Merydith.
      p.   cm.
   Includes index.
   ISBN 0-7615-0794-9
   1. Bread.   2. Automatic bread machines.   I. Title.
   TX769.M45   1996
   641.8' 15—dc20   96-39094
                                                 CIP

96 97 98 99 00 01 HH 10 9 8 7 6 5 4 3 2 1
Printed in the United States of America

How to Order
Single copies may be ordered from Prima Publishing, P.O. Box 1260BK, Rocklin, CA 95677; telephone (916) 632-4400. Quantity discounts are also available. On your letterhead, include information concerning the intended use of the books and the number of books you wish to purchase.

Visit us online at http://www.primapublishing.com

This book is dedicated to my mother-in-law, Jane Mae Merydith, who introduced me to the delightful joys of making home-made bread.

Contents

Creating Sourdough
169

Introduction

The word "seasons" brings different pictures to our mind . . . there are seasons in our lives, seasons in our moods, seasons in the weather . . . and for each of these seasons there is change. In our lives, we change from child to teenager to adult. Our moods can shift from sadness to joy to relief. So too, the weather changes during the year. We have memories of past seasons, enjoy the uniqueness of each, and look forward to winter, spring, summer, and autumn coming again. This book of bread-machine recipes reflects the yearly seasons by using ingredients and garden produce that provoke seasonal joys.

Seasons define for us the types of foods that we cook and eat. Winter, with its cold weather and clear colors, is full of produce that has been dried or sugared. We celebrate the holidays with pine and spices, rich, hearty meals, and the warmth of indoor fires. Spring is filled with new plants, a freshness in color and foods . . . herbs, strawberries, lemons, and oranges. Spring is a new beginning, and we crave young tender peas and greens, along with lighter meals. Summer is the warm-weather time of tomatoes, corn, melons, berries, and zucchini; it is an abundant, relaxed season full of picnics and barbecues. Autumn brings the soft-hued browns and reds of dried leaves, pumpkins, apples, nuts, and a desire to celebrate our thankfulness for the blessings around us.

Throughout the years, the process of making bread has always been time consuming yet rewarding. Today, as time management seems to invade all parts of our lives, bread making has not been easy to fit into our days. What a difference the bread machine makes! It gives us homemade bread with rich flavor and healthful nutrients, filling the physical and emotional needs of the baker and the partaker. The bread machine handles the time-consuming process of kneading, rising, and baking the bread. The machine can even be set with a timer for the aroma and taste of fresh-baked bread when you want it.

Baking bread with the bread machine is simplicity itself: Choose a recipe, measure the ingredients into the bread pan, select a baking cycle, and in a few hours' time you'll have a freshly baked loaf. Fresh bread is nutritious and flavorful and has that just-baked goodness. The following recipes are easy to understand, quick to put together, and enjoyable to eat.

A Few Hints for Baking with Bread Machines

The market has a number of different bread machines available. Some machines have features that include cycle selections, loaf sizes and types, and ease of cleaning. There are specific directions for each machine. Follow those for your particular machine to ensure success. If you have yet to get a machine, it is best to check around with friends, stores, and library resources for the machine that has the features you want. Note that machines with a small viewing window produce an evenly browned crust whereas machines that have the larger bubble windows work better if the window is covered on the inside with aluminum foil.

Carefully follow your machine's instructions for adding recipe ingredients. This will affect the outcome of your bread. Each brand of bread machine will stir and knead somewhat differently; consequently, the order of ingredients is important. In this book of recipes, liquids are listed first, then dry ingredients, and the yeast is added last. It is important that the yeast does not come into contact with the liquids until the machine begins mixing. If fruit and/or nuts are part of the recipe, they are added before the yeast, unless your machine has a fruit and nut bread cycle. The process works best when the ingredients sit for about 10 minutes in the bread pan before starting the machine. The closer that cold ingredients come to room temperature, the more the action of the yeast is encouraged.

The choice of the baking cycle varies with the size of loaf and types of flour used. The recipes in this book specify the size of the finished loaf and the suggested baking time. This information, along with the type of flour used, should give you enough information to select the correct baking cycle on any machine.

Moisture or dryness of a loaf is determined by the amount of liquid and flour in the bread pan. As the machine begins to stir and knead the dough, some water or flour may need to be added to make the dough correct. The easiest way is to add 1 tablespoon of water or flour at a time; watching to see how the dough is responding. These additions should not amount to more than a couple of tablespoons. The dough should be smooth, not crumbly, holding its shape in a nicely rounded form. It should not be sticking to the sides of the pan.

These recipes have been made successfully using a bread machine, but because each machine may not work exactly as another, slight corrections may be necessary.

The ingredients listed in these recipes can all be found in grocery stores. The wheat bran, rye flour, and oat flour can usually be found in the health food section. Bulgur is usually found by the rice. If your grocery store does not have some of these items, then a health food or natural food store would be the best place to check.

Sourdough bread recipes are made with a *sourdough starter.* These starters are available in stores (usually in the specialty section), or there is the option of making your own. I have included a starter recipe at the back of the book (see page 173), which uses the bacteria contained in yogurt to create a hardy, stable starter.

You will note that only a small amount of salt is used in these breads, but even that is not necessary if you are on a low-sodium diet.

The yeast used for these recipes is the dry yeast packaged in packets containing 2 1/4 teaspoons each. Be sure to check the expiration date on the package to ensure healthy, active yeast.

Another important fact is that diet margarine or butter is not used as an ingredient in these recipes. Regular margarine or butter should be used because they have a lower moisture content than the diet types. This difference in moisture can cause the bread to fall as it is baking, so be sure to use only regular butter or margarine.

For ease in measuring honey or molasses, first measure the oil or melted butter in the same utensil—a tablespoon—creating a slick surface for these sticky ingredients to slip off of quickly. Canola oil was used for these recipes, but you may substitute another oil as long as it is a salad oil.

After the bread has finished baking, it is best to let it cool before slicing. The bread should be placed on a rack while cooling to prevent moisture collecting and causing sogginess. This allows the bread to firm in texture just enough so that a knife can slice through cleanly. If the loaf is coarse-textured, it is easier to slice vertically down the middle of the bread and then slice horizontally into thick slices.

When the bread is completely cooled, it should be packaged in an airtight container or Ziploc bag and stored in the refrigerator. This prevents the bread from molding because there are no preservatives present. The bread may also be placed in the freezer for long-term storage of 3 months or so, if it is properly wrapped in heavy-duty foil or a freezer Ziploc bag. To use the frozen bread, take it out of the freezer, let it thaw at room temperature, and then warm it in the oven for 10 minutes before serving, or heat it in the microwave for about 20 seconds a slice.

As to the cost-effectiveness of a bread machine versus store-purchased loaves, I've found that the ingredients by themselves are not more than that of a loaf of bread. The cost of the machine is eventually absorbed as the months of bread baking accumulate—it doesn't take long. And it is such an enjoyable pastime, with results that far exceed store-bought bread.

This book is divided into sections coinciding with the seasons of the year. Of course, all of these breads may be made during any time of the year, but they serve as a welcome exclamation point to the particular season in which they are found.

With each recipe, be sure to enjoy the flavors, smells, and colors of the individual seasons as baked in these breads.

Winter

Winter brings a stark, frigid landscape, trees and bushes without leaves, dark, low clouds swollen with rain, and cold, whistling winds. But inside we bolster our spirits with brilliant holiday colors, the warmth of an indoor fire, spices that perfume the air, sweet rolls for a good-morning treat, the silver and gold of tinsel and ornaments, and twinkling, sparkling lights.

During this time of year, cooking and baking add comfort to our souls and our bodies. Bread is a hearty delight joined with soups, stews, roast turkeys, hot cocoa, or a pot of tea to bring us warmth and sustenance.

The recipes in this winter selection include robust breads such as Whole Wheat Molasses Bread, Cinnamon-Walnut Bread, Sourdough Wheat and Grain Bread, and deep, dark Raisin-Pumpernickel Bread. The Cashew-Date Bread resembles a fruit cake in texture and moistness, with the added flavor and lightness of a yeast bread. Chile-Cheese Bread is perfect with a hot stew or enchiladas, while Potato-Wheat Bread is satisfying with any type of hot meal on a cold winter's evening. Holiday choices include the Citrus Celebration Bread and the Portuguese Sweet Bread. The Monkey Bread, Surprise Cinnamon Rolls, or Swedish Cardamom Braid make a delicious beginning to Christmas and New Year's mornings. Try them all to enhance your meals during the cold winter months.

Tasty Wheat Bread

Sometimes a whole wheat bread can be bitter, so unbleached flour is added to this recipe to soften that taste. The honey gives it a little sweetness and the powdered milk adds some richness. It is a fairly even-textured loaf, moist and firm, and can be sliced into nice thick pieces for sandwiches or toast, or warmed to go with dinner. It is a versatile bread with great homemade flavor.

1 1/4　cups water
1　　　tablespoon canola oil
2　　　tablespoons honey
2　　　cups unbleached flour
1 3/4　cups whole wheat flour
2　　　tablespoons nonfat dry milk
1　　　teaspoon salt
2 1/4　teaspoons (1 package) dry yeast

Measure the water, oil, and honey into the bread pan. Next add the unbleached flour, whole wheat flour, dry milk, and salt. Make a well in the dry ingredients and pour the yeast into the well. Select the basic whole wheat bread cycle for a 1- to 1 1/2-pound loaf. The baking time will be about 45 minutes.

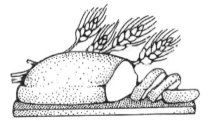

Potato Bread

The potato produces a moist, even-textured loaf with a beautiful, crunchy, light-brown crust. The flavor is the yeasty, down-home goodness of just-baked bread.

1	medium potato
$^{1}/_{2}$	cup milk
$^{3}/_{4}$	cup water
3	cups unbleached flour
1	teaspoon salt
1	teaspoon dry yeast

Bake or microwave a medium potato until tender. Peel the skin and then grate the potato until you have about $^{3}/_{4}$ cup (lightly packed). Measure the water and the milk into the bread pan. Next add the flour, the potato, and the salt. Make a well in the dry ingredients and add the yeast. Select the basic bread cycle for a 1- to 1$^{1}/_{2}$-pound loaf, with a baking time of about 45 minutes.

Whole Wheat Molasses Bread

This bread bakes up to a beautiful golden brown. It is satisfyingly moist, with a nice even texture. The tantalizing smell of molasses and wheat as it bakes makes it difficult to wait for the loaf to cool to cutting temperature. This bread can be used for sandwiches or toasted and spread with butter and/or honey.

$^3/_4$ cup water
$^1/_3$ cup milk
3   tablespoons melted butter
3   tablespoons molasses
1 $^3/_4$ cups whole wheat flour
2   cups all-purpose flour
2   tablespoons sugar
1   teaspoon salt
2 $^1/_4$ teaspoons (1 package) dry yeast

Measure the water, milk, butter, and molasses into the bread pan. Next measure in the wheat flour, all-purpose flour, sugar, and salt. Make a well in the dry ingredients and pour in the yeast. Select the basic whole wheat bread cycle for a 1- to 1$^1/_2$-pound loaf. The baking time will be approximately 45 minutes.

Cinnamon-Walnut Bread

You will smell the delicious aroma of cinnamon as this bread bakes. The loaf is moist with an even texture and a lovely soft brown crust, and it tastes as good as it smells. It is satisfying toasted for breakfast or an evening snack. It keeps well either in the refrigerator or the freezer.

½   cup water
1   cup milk
6   tablespoons melted butter
4½ cups all-purpose flour
3   tablespoons sugar
1   teaspoon salt
3   teaspoons cinnamon
½   cup finely chopped walnuts
1½ teaspoons dry yeast

Measure the water, milk, and melted butter into the bread pan. Then add the flour, sugar, salt, cinnamon, and walnuts. Make a well in the dry ingredients and add the yeast. Select the basic bread cycle for a 2-pound loaf, with a baking time of about 50 minutes. If your machine has a cycle in which you add the nuts later, follow the specific directions for your machine.

Malted Barley Bread

This bread has a mild wheat and malted-barley flavor, with a hint of sweetness. The compact loaf has a moist even texture and makes solid sandwiches and crunchy toast.

Cereal Mixture

1   cup nutty barley cereal (such as Grape Nuts)
2   tablespoons honey
1   cup warm water

Dough

$^1/_2$ cup water
2   tablespoons canola oil
3   cups all-purpose flour
6   tablespoons nonfat dry milk
1   teaspoon salt
$^1/_8$ teaspoon powdered ginger
$2^1/_4$ teaspoons (1 package) dry yeast

Combine the first three ingredients and let the cereal mixture stand 30 minutes.

Measure the water and oil into the bread pan. Add the cereal mixture. Next add the flour, dry milk, salt, and ginger. Make a well in the dry ingredients and add the yeast. Choose the basic bread cycle for a 2-pound loaf. The baking time will be about 50 minutes.

Portuguese Sweet Bread

This cake-like bread makes a lovely dessert. It has a dark crust and a very dense, moist middle that is sweet and rich with eggs. It is mouthwatering served warm with coffee after a meal and excellent topped with fruits, and their juices, which soak into this bread's soft, rich, spongy center.

¹/₄	cup water
¹/₃	cup melted butter, cooled
¹/₃	cup milk
3	eggs, lightly beaten
3²/₃	cups all-purpose flour
¹/₂	cup sugar
1	teaspoon salt
2	teaspoons dry yeast

Measure the water, butter, milk, and eggs into the bread pan. Then measure in the flour, sugar, and salt. Make a well in the dry ingredients and put the yeast into the well. Select the basic bread cycle for a 1- to 1¹/₂-pound loaf. Baking time will be about 40 minutes.

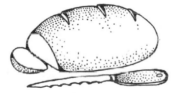

Raisin Pumpernickel Bread

This bread is dark and dense with a smooth, deep pumpernickel flavor. The moist loaf, filled with healthful ingredients, is excellent toasted or thickly sliced to hold deli-sandwich makings.

1 1/4 cups water
1   tablespoon canola oil
1/4   cup dark molasses
1   cup rye flour
1   cup whole wheat flour
1 1/2 cups all-purpose flour
2   tablespoons unsweetened cocoa
1   tablespoon instant coffee powder
2   tablespoons cornmeal
1/2   teaspoon salt
1/2   cup raisins
2 1/4 teaspoons (1 package) dry yeast

Add the water, oil, and molasses to the bread pan. Next
measure in the rye, whole wheat, and all-purpose flours. Then
add the cocoa, instant coffee, cornmeal, salt, and raisins.
Make a well in the dry ingredients and add the yeast. Select
the basic whole wheat bread cycle for a 1- to 1 1/2-pound loaf.
Baking time will be approximately 45 minutes.

Cheddar Cheese Bread

Baking to a fine even texture, this solid loaf has a delicate cheese flavor, a nice crisp crust, and a moist center. It's great toasted and adds a subtle cheese-flavored dimension to a sandwich.

3/4   cup milk
1   tablespoon honey
1/2   cup water
3 3/4   cups all-purpose flour
1   teaspoon dry mustard
1/8   teaspoon cayenne pepper
1   teaspoon salt
3/4   cup grated cheddar cheese
2 1/4   teaspoons (1 package) dry yeast

Measure the milk, honey, and water into the bread pan. Then add the flour, mustard, cayenne pepper, salt, and cheddar cheese. Make a well in the dry ingredients and add the yeast. Select the basic bread cycle for a 2-pound loaf. The baking time will be about 50 minutes.

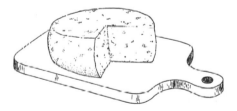

Sourdough Wheat and Grain Bread

Moist on the inside, brown and crunchy on the outside, this bread has a rich, hearty, whole-grain flavor and a sturdy, dense texture. It is great for sandwiches, with dinner, or toasted for breakfast with lots of jam.

²/₃   cup Sourdough Starter (see page 173),
       room temperature
1   cup milk
2   tablespoons water
3   tablespoons honey
1   egg, lightly beaten
1   tablespoon melted butter
1   cup whole wheat flour
2²/₃   cups all-purpose flour
1   teaspoon salt
¹/₄   cup rolled oats
¹/₄   cup bulgur
¹/₄   cup cornmeal
²/₃   cup unprocessed bran
1   teaspoon dry yeast

Pour the sourdough starter, milk, water, honey, egg, and melted butter into the bread pan. Add the whole wheat flour, all-purpose flour, salt, rolled oats, bulgur, cornmeal, and unprocessed bran. Make a well in the dry ingredients and measure in the yeast. Select the basic bread cycle for a 2-pound loaf. Baking time will be about 50 minutes.

Nutty Nutritious Bread

*The final product is a wonderfully firm, solid
bread that is excellent for sandwiches and toast. It
bakes up to a rich golden brown with a crunchy,
chewy texture and a mild flavor of sunflower seed
and honey. This is a satisfying and wholesome
bread for a cold winter's day.*

1 1/2 cups water
1/4   cup honey
2   tablespoons canola oil
1 1/2 cups whole wheat flour
3   cups unbleached flour
1   teaspoon salt
1/4   cup wheat germ
1/4   cup sunflower seeds
2   tablespoons sesame seeds
2   tablespoons wheat bran
1   tablespoon bulgur
1   teaspoon dry yeast

Measure the water, honey, and oil into the bread pan.
Next measure in the flours, salt, wheat germ, sunflower seeds,
sesame seeds, wheat bran, and bulgur. Make a well in the dry
ingredients and add the yeast. Select the basic whole wheat
bread cycle for a 2-pound loaf, with a baking time of about
55 minutes.

Citrus Celebration Bread

Serve this beautiful bread for dessert or toasted for breakfast. It bakes to a nice tall loaf, which is very moist, even-textured, and sweet. The crunchy citrus rinds burst with flavor in each delicious bite.

1/4	cup milk
1/3	cup water
6	tablespoons melted butter
2	eggs, lightly beaten
4	cups all-purpose flour
1/3	cup sugar
1/2	teaspoon salt
1/4	teaspoon nutmeg
1/2	teaspoon cinnamon
1	tablespoon grated lemon rind
1	tablespoon grated orange rind
1/3	cup currants
1/3	cup chopped almonds
1	teaspoon dry yeast

Measure the milk, water, melted butter, and lightly beaten eggs into the bread pan. Next add the flour, sugar, salt, nutmeg, cinnamon, lemon and orange rinds, currants, and nuts. If your machine has a particular time to add the currants and nuts, then follow those directions. Make a well in the dry ingredients and add the yeast. Select the basic bread cycle for a 2-pound loaf. Baking time will be about 50 minutes.

Sour Rye

This sturdy loaf is dense with an even texture. The crust is crunchy; the middle moist. It cuts easily into nice thick slices for sandwiches and has a good sour rye flavor that goes well with any type of lunch meat.

$^1/_2$	cup Sourdough Starter (see page 173), room temperature
1	cup water
2	tablespoons canola oil
1	tablespoon molasses
$1^1/_2$	cups rye flour
$2^1/_4$	cups unbleached flour
1	teaspoon salt
$2^1/_4$	teaspoons (1 package) dry yeast

Measure the sourdough starter, water, oil, and molasses into the bread pan. Add the rye flour, unbleached flour, and salt. Make a well in the dry ingredients and measure in the yeast. Select the basic bread cycle for a 1- to $1^1/_2$-pound loaf. Baking time will be approximately 40 minutes.

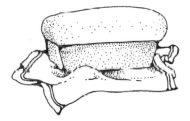

Cracked Wheat and Raisin Bread

A wholesome, satisfying bread for sandwiches or morning toast, this recipe bakes into a beautiful soft loaf with an uneven texture and a crunchy, nutty flavor from the cracked wheat. It slices well after it has cooled completely.

1 ¹/₃ cups water
1   tablespoon melted butter
3   cups all-purpose flour
³/₄   cup cracked wheat or bulgur
¹/₄   cup brown sugar
1   teaspoon salt
¹/₂   cup raisins
2 ¹/₄ teaspoons (1 package) dry yeast

Pour the water and melted butter into the bread pan. Next add the all-purpose flour, cracked wheat, brown sugar, salt, and raisins. Make a well in the dry ingredients and measure the yeast into the well. If your machine has a timer for adding raisins, then follow those directions. Select the basic bread cycle for a 1- to 1¹/₂-pound loaf. Baking time will be about 40 minutes.

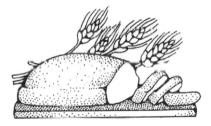

Potato Wheat Bread

*Moist, with a smooth potato and wheat flavor,
this loaf finishes to a nice even texture. Light and
airy and easy to slice, it also keeps well. This is
good toasted or as a sandwich bread.*

1   medium potato, boiled and mashed (see below)
1 1/2 cups cooled potato water (see below)
3   tablespoons canola oil
3   tablespoons honey
2 1/2 cups whole wheat flour
1 1/4 cups unbleached flour
2   tablespoons nonfat dry milk
1   teaspoon salt
1   teaspoon dry yeast

Peel the potato and boil until soft. Remove the potato from the potato water (save this) and mash to get 2/3 cup (lightly packed). Let the potato water cool and measure out, adding tap water if necessary to make 1 1/2 cups. Pour the potato water into the bread pan. Add the oil, honey, and mashed potato. Next measure in the whole wheat and unbleached flours, nonfat dry milk, and salt. Make a well in the dry ingredients and measure in the yeast. Select the basic whole wheat bread cycle for a 1- to 1 1/2-pound loaf. Baking time will be about 45 minutes.

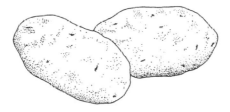

Sourdough Whole Wheat Bread

Sourdough tends to create a moist, flavorful bread. This particular loaf is soft and even-textured with a hint of molasses mingled with the sourdough. It bakes to a deep brown and is excellent toasted and spread with butter, honey, or jam. It holds together well for sandwiches and is an excellent accompaniment for dinner.

³/₄ cup Sourdough Starter (see page 173),
     room temperature
³/₄ cup milk
¹/₄ cup molasses
6 tablespoons canola oil
3³/₄ cups whole wheat flour
¹/₄ teaspoon baking soda
1 teaspoon salt
1 teaspoon dry yeast

Measure the sourdough starter, milk, molasses, and oil into
the bread pan. Next measure in the flour, baking soda, and
salt. Make a well in the dry ingredients and measure the yeast
into the well. Select the basic whole wheat bread cycle for a
1- to 1¹/₂-pound loaf. Baking time will be about 45 minutes.

Surprise Cinnamon Rolls

This extremely workable dough is made with cottage cheese. It bakes into light and airy sweet rolls, which are full of protein for a good breakfast. You can adjust the amount of cinnamon filling in this recipe to produce sweeter or not-so-sweet rolls. Either way, these rolls are incredibly yummy.

DOUGH

5	tablespoons water
1	cup lowfat cottage cheese, room temperature
2	eggs, lightly beaten
1/4	cup melted butter
3	cups all-purpose flour
1/4	cup sugar
1	teaspoon salt
2 1/4	teaspoons (1 package) dry yeast

CINNAMON FILLING

4	tablespoons butter
9	tablespoons brown sugar
1	teaspoon cinnamon

To make the dough: Measure the water, cottage cheese, eggs, and melted butter into the bread pan. Add flour, sugar, and salt. Make a well in the dry ingredients and measure in the yeast. Set the bread machine for dough cycle only, or if your machine does not have this cycle, stop the machine after the dough has risen once. Take the dough out of the machine and lay it onto a floured board. Work the dough with your hands to expel all of the bubbles.

In a 13 × 9 inch baking pan, melt 2 tablespoons of the butter. Spread evenly around the bottom of the pan. Sprinkle 3 tablespoons of the brown sugar evenly over the butter. Divide the dough into 2 portions. Roll each portion, one at a time (you may need to use a little flour on your rolling pin) into a rectangle, about 13 × 9 inches. Brush the rectangle with 1 tablespoon of melted butter. Sprinkle 3 tablespoons of the brown sugar over the buttered dough, and then about ½ teaspoon of the cinnamon over the brown sugar. With your fingers, gently roll the dough along its length, forming a "jelly" roll. Press the long edge of dough snugly onto the roll. Lightly flour a sharp knife and cut the roll into 8 portions. Put each portion into the baking pan, spacing evenly between each roll.

Repeat the process with the second portion of dough. Cover the pan with plastic wrap and cloth and place it in a warm spot for about 40 minutes or until the rolls have doubled in size.

Bake in a preheated 375-degree oven for about 15 minutes.

When the cinnamon rolls are done, wait about 5 minutes, then run a knife around the edge of the pan. Turn the rolls out onto racks or wax paper to cool. A glaze of ¾ cup confectioners sugar and 1 to 2 tablespoons water may be drizzled over the top of the rolls.

To store, place in an airtight container after the rolls have completely cooled. These may be frozen and used later by bringing them to room temperature and warming them in the microwave or oven.

Note: Chopped walnuts and/or raisins may be sprinkled over the cinnamon filling on the dough before rolling. This will add to the flavor, texture, and nutrition.

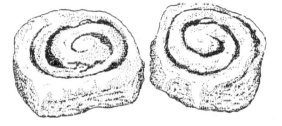

Chile-Cheese Bread

Bring the aroma and pungent flavors of Southwestern cooking to your table with this moist, sturdy bread. The flavor enhances any type of sandwich makings; it's a unique spicy treat.

1 1/4 cups water
3 3/4 cups unbleached flour
1   teaspoon sugar
1   teaspoon salt
1   teaspoon ground cumin
1   cup grated cheddar cheese, chilled
1/4   cup diced green chiles
1   teaspoon dry yeast

Pour the water into the bread pan. Next add the flour, sugar, salt, cumin, cheddar cheese, and chiles. Make a well in the dry ingredients and measure in the yeast. Select the basic bread cycle for a 1- to 1 1/2-pound loaf. Baking time will be about 40 minutes.

Wheat Spice Bread

Wonderful for breakfast, toasted and spread with butter and honey, this bread has a smooth cardamom and nutmeg flavor. It bakes to a fine, even-textured loaf, with a poppy seed crunch in a tender, moist slice.

1	tablespoon molasses
1	tablespoon melted butter
$^2/_3$	cup milk
6	tablespoons water
1 $^1/_3$	cups all-purpose flour
2	cups whole wheat flour
1	teaspoon poppy seeds
$^1/_2$	teaspoon cardamom
$^1/_2$	teaspoon nutmeg
2	teaspoons sugar
1	teaspoon salt
1	teaspoon dry yeast

Pour the molasses, melted butter, milk, and water into the bread pan. Next add the flours, spices, sugar, and salt. Make a well in the dry ingredients and measure in the yeast. Select the basic whole wheat bread cycle for a 1- to 1 $^1/_2$-pound loaf. Baking time will be about 45 minutes.

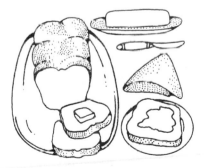

Cashew Date Bread

The dates give this dense loaf an exceptional moistness and sweetness. The flavors of cinnamon, cashews, and dates intermingle, creating a rich, dessert-like bread. Excellent for company coffee or as a brunch/tea bread.

1   tablespoon molasses
1   cup + 1 tablespoon water
3   tablespoons canola oil
3³/₄ cups whole wheat flour
¹/₂ teaspoon salt
1   teaspoon cinnamon
¹/₂ cup chopped unsalted cashews or walnuts
¹/₂ cup chopped pitted dates
2¹/₄ teaspoons (1 package) dry yeast

Measure the molasses, water, and oil into the bread pan. Add the whole wheat flour, salt, cinnamon, cashews, and dates. If your machine has a cycle for fruit and nut bread, then add these two ingredients when the machine's directions indicate. Make a well in the dry ingredients and measure in the yeast. Select the basic bread cycle or the fruit and nut bread cycle for a 1- to 1¹/₂-pound loaf. Baking time will be about 40 minutes.

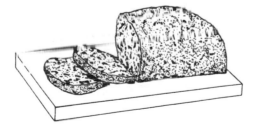

Whole Wheat Bagels

These bagels bake to a pretty golden brown. They are crunchy on the outside, nice and moist on the inside, and very chewy, with a wholesome whole wheat flavor. The honey keeps the whole wheat from being bitter and adds sweetness. These bagels are an excellent breakfast all by themselves or as part of a bigger all-encompassing brunch. They also make good sturdy sandwiches and a nutritious snack.

1   cup milk
2   tablespoons honey
1   egg, lightly beaten
2   tablespoons melted butter
$3^3/_4$ cups whole wheat flour
1   teaspoon salt
$2^1/_4$ teaspoons (1 package) dry yeast

Measure the milk, honey, egg, and melted butter into the bread pan. Then add the whole wheat flour and salt. Make a well in the dry ingredients and measure in the yeast. Select the dough cycle on the bread machine. If your machine does not have this cycle, then select the basic bread cycle and stop the machine after the dough has risen once.

Turn the dough out onto a floured board. Evenly cut the dough into 12 pieces and then shape these into 12 balls. Poke a hole in the middle of each ball, pulling gently to enlarge the hole and working each into a doughnut-like shape. Place on an ungreased cookie sheet. Cover lightly with a dry cloth and let rise for 30 minutes.

In a large kettle, combine 2 quarts water and $^1/_4$ teaspoon salt. Bring to a boil, add 3 to 4 bagels to the kettle, and cook for 6 minutes on each side. Remove with a slotted spoon and place on an ungreased baking sheet.

When all 12 bagels have been boiled, bake at 375 degrees for 20 to 25 minutes. Place the baked bagels on a wire rack and allow to cool completely before storing. A gallon-size Ziploc bag works well and can also be used as a container when freezing the fresh bagels. To warm frozen bagels, place one bagel in the microwave and heat for about 45 seconds on high.

Oatmeal-Molasses Rolls

Light, tender, and moist, these rolls are very tasty. They have a slightly sweet, rich flavor with a hint of molasses. After these rolls have cooled completely, they can be frozen in a Ziploc bag for longer storage.

1	cup water
2	tablespoons melted butter
2	tablespoons molasses
1	egg, lightly beaten
3 3/4	cups + 2 tablespoons all-purpose flour
1/2	cup oats
1/2	cup firmly packed brown sugar
1/2	teaspoon salt
2 1/4	teaspoons (1 package) dry yeast

Measure the water, melted butter, molasses, and egg into the bread pan. Add the flour, oats, brown sugar, and salt. Make a well in the dry ingredients and measure in the yeast. Select the dough cycle. If your machine does not have this option, choose the basic bread cycle and stop the machine after the dough has risen once.

Turn the dough out onto a floured board. With floured hands, divide the dough into 18 even pieces, forming each into a ball. Place these in a greased 13 × 9 inch baking pan. Cover and let rise until doubled in size, about 1 hour. Heat the oven to 375 degrees, and bake for 20 to 25 minutes, or until golden brown. The baked rolls may be brushed with melted butter.

Swedish Cardamom Braid

Served warm, the wonderful flavor of cardamom infuses this slightly sweet braided bread. It bakes to a golden brown with a light fluffy texture in the middle. The braid can be cut into slices or you can simply tear off a piece if the bread is still warm. This is a treat for breakfast, warmed with fruit sliced over the top. It can be frozen successfully for an upcoming brunch buffet.

²/₃	cup milk
6	tablespoons water
¹/₃	cup + 2 tablespoons melted butter
1	egg, lightly beaten
4 ¹/₂	cups all-purpose flour
¹/₂	cup sugar
1	teaspoon salt
¹/₂	teaspoon cardamom
2 ¹/₄	teaspoons (1 package) dry yeast

Measure the milk, water, ¹/₃ cup melted butter, and egg into
the bread pan. Add the flour, sugar, salt, and cardamom. Make
a well in the dry ingredients and pour the yeast into the well.
Select the dough cycle, or if your machine does not have this
option, select the basic bread cycle and stop the machine after
the dough has risen once.

Turn out the dough onto a floured board. Divide the dough
into 3 equal pieces. Roll each piece between your hands until
it becomes a rope about 17 inches long and place on a greased
cookie sheet. Make a braid using the 3 ropes, working from
one end to the other. Press the 3 pieces at each end together
snugly. Brush the braid with 1 tablespoon melted butter. Cover
with plastic wrap and let rise in a warm place until doubled in
size, about 40 to 60 minutes.

Preheat the oven to 375 degrees and bake the braid for 20
minutes. Brush with the remaining 1 tablespoon melted butter
when it is finished baking and sprinkle with some granulated
sugar. Cool on a wire rack.

Hearty Garlic Bread

This bread bakes into a small, sturdy, even-textured loaf. It has a hearty garlic flavor, with the herbs adding dimension to the overall taste. This bread is very aromatic as it is baking and when warmed or toasted. It is delicious buttered or spread with cream cheese and livens up any sandwich meat or spread. You'll find it makes a wonderful accompaniment to Italian dishes.

1 cup + 3 tablespoons milk
2 tablespoons molasses
1 tablespoon canola oil
3 cups whole wheat flour
³/₄ cup oats
¹/₂ teaspoon dried basil
¹/₂ teaspoon dried oregano
¹/₂ teaspoon garlic powder
¹/₂ teaspoon salt (optional)
2 ¹/₄ teaspoons (1 package) dry yeast

Measure the milk, molasses, and oil into the bread pan. Add the whole wheat flour, oats, basil, oregano, garlic powder, and salt. Make a well in the dry ingredients and add the yeast. Select the basic bread cycle for a 1- to 1 ¹/₂-pound loaf. Baking time will be approximately 40 minutes.

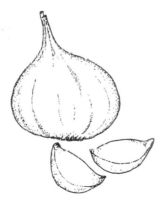

Monkey Bread

Easy to work with, this dough bakes up delicate, sweet, and mouthwatering. Each bite-sized, pull-apart portion is covered with cinnamon, brown sugar, and butter. It's best served warm but can be sliced and warmed in the microwave at a later time.

Raisins, currants, and/or chopped nuts can be sprinkled over each layer as it is put in the pan to add flavor and nutrition. Serve this for breakfast or with coffee.

The Dough

¹/₂ cup water
¹/₄ cup melted butter, cooled
³/₄ cup milk
2 eggs, lightly beaten
4¹/₂ cups all-purpose flour
¹/₂ cup sugar
1 teaspoon salt
2¹/₄ teaspoons (1 package) dry yeast

The Filling

¹/₃ cup brown sugar
1 teaspoon cinnamon
¹/₃ cup melted butter

To make the dough: Measure the water, melted butter, eggs, and milk into the bread pan. Add the flour, sugar, and salt. Make a well in the dry ingredients and add the yeast. Select the dough cycle, or if your machine does not have that selection, select the basic bread cycle and stop the machine after the dough has risen once. After the dough has risen, punch it down and let it rest for about 10 minutes on a floured board.

Butter a tube or bundt cake pan. To prepare the filling. Combine in a small bowl the brown sugar, the cinnamon, and the ¹/₃ cup melted butter. Pinch off enough dough to make a golf-sized ball. Roll the ball in the brown-sugar mixture and place in the bottom of the tube pan. Continue with all of the dough, lining the bottom of the pan first, and then arranging the rest of the balls in loose layers. Pour any leftover brown-sugar mixture over the top. Cover loosely with plastic wrap and let rise to the top of the pan, about 40 minutes.

Preheat the oven to 375 degrees and bake for 45 minutes to an hour. If the top of the bread is beginning to get too dark, place foil over it. This bread must be cooked completely all the way through. Tap the top of the bread and listen for a hollow sound.

Unmold the bread immediately when it is done cooking. This is delectable when eaten warm by pulling pieces off of the whole. If you wish to slice the bread, let it cool completely first.

 Spring

Many shades of green and watercolor pastels; the smell of freshly tilled and cultivated ground; new leaves on the trees, new buds on the vines; the clean crispness of a spring shower; fluffy clouds in a blue, blue sky; the drip, drip of melting snow.

Spring is a time of new beginnings. Spring brings a lightness to our steps as we see bright daffodils and tulips and feel the gentle breezes. Spring is a time of celebration, a time of resurrection and new life.

Spring's colors and flavors are prevalent in this season's selection of breads for your bread machine. The light golden color of the Honey-Yogurt Oat Bread, the yellow crunchiness of the Colonial Bread, and the tender beauty of the Poppy Seed Ring evoke the essence of springtime and the newness of life around us. The Orange-Craisin Bread wakes up our taste buds; the Sourdough Bagels are an essential for picnics as the weather warms. The Prosciutto Bread makes a sandwich by itself, with the meat and cheese baked right into the loaf. It packs quickly for those out-of-the-way, on-the-road lunches when spring fever hits. Celebrate spring and enjoy the following recipes.

Wonderful White Bread

This loaf is dense, moist, and flavorful with just a hint of sweetness. It is great for toast, sandwiches, or to use with any food that you want to sop up to the last drop . . . a good sturdy bread for dunking.

1   cup milk
2   tablespoons water
2   teaspoons canola oil
1   tablespoon honey
3 ¹/₄ cups all-purpose flour
1   teaspoon salt
1   teaspoon dry yeast

..., oil, and honey into the bread
... flour and salt. Make a well in the dry ingredients
and measure in the yeast. Select the basic bread cycle for a 1-
to 1¹/₂-pound loaf. The baking time will be about 40 minutes.

Sourdough Bagels

Excellent for breakfast with cream cheese or jam, these sourdough bagels bake to a golden brown crust with a soft, tender middle. The sourdough provides a tangy flavor and extra moisture. These also are wonderful for lunch sandwiches and as a nutritious, filling snack. This recipe makes 12 medium bagels.

1 egg, lightly beaten
2 tablespoons melted butter
$^1/_2$ cup Sourdough Starter (see page 173),
room temperature
$^3/_4$ cup milk
$3^3/_4$ cups all-purpose flour
2 teaspoons sugar
1 teaspoon salt
$2^1/_4$ teaspoons (1 package) dry yeast

Measure the egg, melted butter, sourdough starter, and milk into the bread pan. Next add the flour, sugar, and salt. Make a well in the dry ingredients and measure in the yeast. Choose the dough cycle on the bread machine. If your machine does not have this option, choose the basic bread cycle and stop the machine after the dough has risen once.

Turn the dough out onto a floured board. Divide the dough evenly into 12 pieces. Roll each piece into a ball, poke a hole in the middle of the ball, and gently stretch the hole so that the dough resembles a doughnut. Place the 12 bagels on a lightly greased cookie sheet. Cover with a cloth and allow the bagels to rise for 30 minutes.

In a large kettle, combine 2 quarts of water and 1 teaspoon sugar. Bring to a boil. Drop two or three of the risen bagels into the boiling water and cook about 4 minutes on each side. Lift out of the water with a slotted utensil and place back onto the cookie sheet. When all 12 bagels have been cooked in the water, preheat the oven to 375 degrees and bake them on the cookie sheet for 20 to 25 minutes. Cool the bagels on a wire rack and store in a Ziploc bag.

White Rice Bread

Uniquely light and airy with a honeycombed texture, this bread is very moist and slightly sweet from the rice. It has a nice old-fashioned feel and smell. This bread is wonderful toasted with butter and jam or honey filling its nooks and crannies. The mild flavor makes it compatible with many foods. It stores very well, either in the fridge or the freezer.

2	cups water
¹/₂	cup raw white rice
3²/₃	cups unbleached flour
1	teaspoon salt
1	teaspoon dry yeast

In a saucepan bring 1 cup water to a boil, add the rice to the water, turn the heat down low, cover the pan, and cook the rice until done, about 20 minutes. Let it cool as you work with the rest of the ingredients.

Measure 1 cup water into the bread pan. Add 3¹/₃ cups of the flour to the pan, reserving ¹/₃ cup. Combine the ¹/₃ cup flour with the cooked rice and stir to cover all of the rice grains. Add this floured rice to the baking pan, then add the salt. Make a well in the ingredients and measure the yeast into the well. Select the basic bread cycle for a 2-pound loaf. Baking time will be approximately 50 minutes.

Orange-Craisin Bread

Craisins are cranberries that have been dried and sweetened. They are a beautiful red and add a little sweetness to this bread, which bakes into a moist, dense, even-textured loaf. The melding of the sweet Craisins with the tangy orange juice, interspersed with the crunchy walnuts, produces a delightful taste sensation. Toast a slice and spread on cream cheese for breakfast or a light lunch. It is also good as a quick pick-me-up for coffee breaks.

1	cup + 1 tablespoon orange juice
1	tablespoon canola oil
1	tablespoon honey
3 $1/4$	cups all-purpose flour
1	teaspoon salt
$1/3$	cup Craisins
$1/3$	cup chopped walnuts
1	teaspoon dry yeast

Measure the orange juice, oil, and honey into the bread pan. Add the flour, salt, Craisins, and walnuts. Make a well in the dry ingredients and add the yeast. Select the basic bread cycle for a 1- to 1 $1/2$-pound loaf. If you have a special cycle for adding fruit and nuts, you may use that selection and add those ingredients when the machine is ready for them. The baking time for this bread should be about 40 minutes.

Sally Lunn

A golden yellow loaf with a light and even texture and the slightly sweet flavor and moistness of an egg bread. Wonderful toasted and spread with jams, honey, or cream cheese, it retains its goodness and moisture for the better part of a week and can also be frozen.

$^1/_2$	cup water
$^1/_2$	cup milk
$^1/_2$	cup (1 stick) melted butter or margarine
3	eggs, lightly beaten
4	cups all-purpose flour
1	teaspoon salt
3	tablespoons granulated sugar
$2^1/_4$	teaspoons (1 package) dry yeast

Measure the water, milk, melted butter, and eggs into the bread pan. Add the flour, salt, and sugar. Make a well in the dry ingredients and measure in the yeast. Select the basic bread cycle for a 2-pound loaf. The baking time will be approximately 50 minutes.

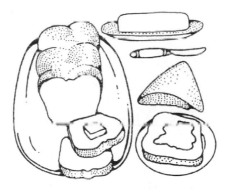

Colonial Bread

The hearty flavor of the rye and wheat flours combined with the crunchiness of the cornmeal creates a very satisfying loaf with a golden brown crust. It has an even texture for easy slicing, which makes it perfect for sandwiches and toast. A great accompaniment to almost any meal, you may find yourself baking this bread every week.

1 1/4 cups water
2   tablespoons canola oil
2 1/2 cups all-purpose flour
6   tablespoons whole wheat flour
1/4   cup rye flour
1/4   cup yellow cornmeal
3   tablespoons brown sugar
1   teaspoon salt
2 1/4 teaspoons (1 package) dry yeast

Measure the water and oil into the bread pan. Add the all-purpose flour, whole wheat flour, rye flour, cornmeal, brown sugar, and salt. Make a well in the dry ingredients and measure in the yeast. Select the basic bread cycle for a 1- to 1 1/2-pound loaf. The baking time will be about 40 minutes.

Anadama Bread

The yellow cornmeal makes this loaf bake to a warm brown color with an excellent smooth flavor and a moist, chewy texture. It is very good toasted with butter and spread with honey or jam for breakfast. It also goes well with soups and stews. This bread freezes well.

1	cup water
3	tablespoons melted butter
$^1/_4$	cup molasses
$4^1/_2$	cups all-purpose flour
$^1/_2$	cup yellow cornmeal
1	teaspoon sugar
$1^1/_2$	teaspoons salt
$2^1/_4$	teaspoons (1 package) dry yeast

Measure the water, melted butter, and molasses into the bread pan. Add the flour, cornmeal, sugar, and salt. Make a well in the dry ingredients and measure in the yeast. Select the basic bread cycle for a 1- to $1^1/_2$-pound loaf, with a baking time of approximately 40 minutes.

Prosciutto Bread

This unique, delicious bread tastes like it takes a lot of work to put together, but it is actually very simple with a bread machine. The bread bakes up moist, light, and even-textured with the subtle flavors of provolone and prosciutto. It's good for snacks, deli sandwiches, or toasted with butter. It's also excellent as a dinner bread and looks beautiful on a buffet table.

³/₄   cup + 2 tablespoons water
2   eggs, beaten
3 ¹/₂ cups all-purpose flour
¹/₈   teaspoon sugar
1   teaspoon salt
¹/₂   teaspoon onion powder
¹/₄   pound prosciutto (fat removed), cut into
      julienne strips
¹/₄   pound provolone cheese, cut into julienne strips
2 ¹/₄ teaspoons (1 package) dry yeast

Measure the water and eggs into the bread pan. Add the flour, sugar, salt, and onion powder. Then add the prosciutto and provolone cheese. Make a well in the dry ingredients and add the yeast. Select the basic bread cycle for a 1- to 1 ¹/₂-pound loaf. Baking time should be about 40 minutes.

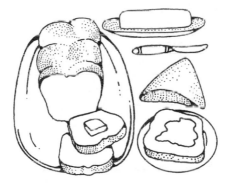

Honey-Cornmeal Bread

The smell and sight of this cornmeal bread as it bakes is mouthwatering. It has a golden crunchy crust and a cornmeal and honey flavor. The texture is coarse with lots of wonderful nooks and crannies for butter to seep into and honey to fill. It is delicious toasted or warmed for dinner.

1/2	cup milk
1/2	cup water
2	tablespoons melted butter
2	tablespoons honey
1 1/3	cups cornmeal
2 1/4	cups unbleached flour
1/2	teaspoon salt
1	teaspoon dry yeast

Measure the milk, water, melted butter, and honey into the bread pan. Add the cornmeal, flour, and salt. Make a well in the dry ingredients and add the yeast. Select the basic bread cycle for a 1- to 1 1/2-pound loaf. Baking time should be about 40 minutes.

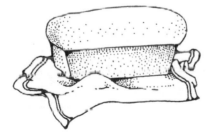

Buttery Whole Wheat Dinner Rolls

Light, tender, and moist, these rolls are great with meals. The combination of the whole wheat flour and the brown sugar brings a depth and richness to the flavor. This recipe makes 24 rolls.

¹/₄   cup water
¹/₂   cup melted butter
1   cup milk
2   eggs, beaten
4¹/₂ cups whole wheat flour
¹/₂   cup brown sugar
1   teaspoon salt
2¹/₄ teaspoons (1 package) dry yeast

Measure the water, melted butter, milk, and eggs into the bread pan. Add the whole wheat flour, brown sugar, and salt. Make a well in the dry ingredients and add the yeast. Select the dough cycle, or if your machine does not have this selection, choose the basic bread cycle and stop the machine after the first rising.

Using a floured board, punch down the dough and cut it into 24 equal pieces. Flatten each piece and fold the dough off-center into the shape of a Parker House roll. Space evenly in large greased baking pan, or on a cookie sheet. Cover with plastic wrap and let rise in a warm place until puffy, about 40 minutes.

Preheat the oven to 350 degrees and bake for 12 to 16 minutes, or until the rolls are soft brown on top.

Granola Wheat Bread

The granola gives a sweet crunch to this delicious, wholesome bread. The loaf is tender with a nice, even texture and is excellent toasted, warmed, or as a bread for delicate sandwiches.

1	cup water
3	tablespoons honey
2	tablespoons canola oil
1	egg, lightly beaten
3	cups whole wheat flour
1	cup granola, broken in small pieces
1	teaspoon salt
2 1/4	teaspoons (1 package) dry yeast

Measure the water, honey, oil, and egg into the bread pan. Add the flour, granola, and salt. Make a well in the dry ingredients and measure in the yeast. Select the basic whole wheat cycle for a 1- to 1 1/2-pound loaf. The baking time will be about 45 minutes.

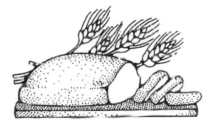

Honey-Yogurt Oat Bread

*The yogurt adds moisture as well as a bit of tang
to this flavorful bread, which has a nice even texture that works well for sandwiches and toast.*

*Small variations on this bread can be made
by using different flavors of yogurt: pineapple,
strawberry, and lemon are flavored yogurts that
work well in this loaf.*

$^1/_4$	cup water
$^3/_4$	cup milk
$^1/_4$	cup plain yogurt
3	tablespoons honey
2	tablespoons melted butter
3	cups whole wheat flour
$^1/_3$	cup rolled oats
1	teaspoon salt
1	teaspoon dry yeast

Measure the water, milk, yogurt, honey, and melted butter into the bread pan. Add the whole wheat flour, rolled oats, and salt. Make a well in the dry ingredients and measure in the yeast. Select the basic whole wheat cycle for a 1 to 1$^1/_2$-pound loaf. Baking time will be about 45 minutes.

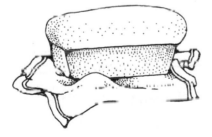

Plain Bagels

This dough is sturdy and handles well. These bagels come out golden brown with a crunchy crust, tender, chewy inside, and classic flavor. This recipe makes 12 medium bagels.

1   cup milk
¹/₄   cup melted butter
1   egg, lightly beaten
3 ³/₄ cups all-purpose flour
1   tablespoon sugar
1   teaspoon salt
2 ¹/₄ teaspoons (1 package) dry yeast

Measure the milk, melted butter, and egg into the bread pan. Add the flour, sugar, and salt. Make a well in the dry ingredients and add the yeast. Select the dough cycle, or if your machine does not have that option, choose the basic bread cycle and stop the machine after the dough has risen once.

Turn the dough out onto a lightly floured board. Divide the dough into 12 equal pieces. Shape the pieces into balls. Make a hole in the middle of each ball, and pull gently to enlarge it, creating a doughnut shape. Place the bagels on an ungreased cookie sheet, cover with a cloth, and let rise for 30 minutes. To help firm the dough, you may chill it for 2 hours, but this is not necessary.

Bring 2 quarts of water and 1 tablespoon sugar to boil and drop the bagels one at a time into the boiling water. Cook about 2 minutes, then turn them over and cook 2 minutes longer. Remove the bagels with a slotted spoon and place them back on the ungreased baking sheet.

Preheat the oven to 375 degrees and bake for 20 to 25 minutes or until golden brown and crisp.

Variations can include poppy seeds, sesame seeds, or herbs sprinkled on top of the bagels before they are baked. Any kind of nut (about ¹/₄ cup, chopped) may be added to the bread pan ingredients as well, for a different taste.

Poppy Seed Ring

This elastic dough is fairly easy to work with. As the directions indicate, the twisting of the dough is simple but a bit messy. The tender, rich dough bakes up beautifully. The amount of poppy seed filling that you use depends on how much of that flavor you desire. I've found that about 1/2 of a 12-ounce can provides a nice subtle touch of poppy seed. This ring makes approximately 16 servings.

THE DOUGH

$^2/_3$ cup water

6 tablespoons melted butter

1 egg, lightly beaten

3$^1/_2$ cups all-purpose flour

$^1/_3$ cup sugar

$^1/_2$ teaspoon salt

2$^1/_4$ teaspoons (1 package) dry yeast

THE FILLING

6 to 12$^1/_2$ ounces canned poppy seed filling (depending on personal taste)

2 tablespoons sugar

THE GLAZE

$^1/_4$ cup confectioners' sugar

1 tablespoon water

Measure the water, melted butter, and egg into the bread pan. Add the flour, sugar, and salt. Make a well in the dry ingredients and add the yeast. Select the dough cycle. If your machine does not have this option, choose the basic bread cycle and stop the machine after the dough has risen once.

Turn the dough onto a floured surface, cover with a cloth, and let it rest about 15 minutes.

Roll dough into a rectangle about 22 × 12 inches. In a small bowl, combine the poppy-seed filling and the 2 tablespoons sugar. Spread this mixture over the dough. Roll up the dough like a jelly roll. Cut roll in half *lengthwise*. Keeping the cut sides up, twist the 2 strands together, then place on an ungreased cookie sheet. Shape into a ring, tucking the ends under to seal. Cover and let rise about 30 minutes, until doubled in size.

Preheat the oven to 350 degrees and bake for 30 minutes. Remove the ring to a wire rack placed over a sheet of waxed paper. In a cup, mix the confectioners' sugar and the 1 tablespoon water. Brush the glaze over the hot ring.

Variations: Spread the dough rectangle with melted butter, brown sugar, cinnamon, and nuts, then roll, cut, and twist. Or mix $^1/_3$ cup sugar with the grated peel of one orange or lemon and sprinkle on the dough; roll, cut, and twist.

Brioche

These rolls bake to a golden brown with shiny
tops and a rich but delicate flavor and texture.
Perfect for breakfast or with a light lunch, the
brioche is a quintessentially French sweet bread.
This recipe makes 24 rolls.

The Dough
¹/₂	cup milk
3	eggs + 1 yolk, lightly beaten
¹/₄	cup water
¹/₂	cup melted butter
4¹/₂	cups all-purpose flour
¹/₃	cup sugar
¹/₂	teaspoon salt
2¹/₄	teaspoons (1 package) dry yeast

The Glaze
1	egg white
1	tablespoon water

Measure the milk, eggs, ¹/₄ cup water, and melted butter into the bread pan. Add the flour, sugar, and salt. Make a well in the dry ingredients and measure in the yeast. Select the dough cycle on the bread machine. If your machine does not have this option, select a basic bread cycle and stop the machine after the dough has risen once.

Turn the dough out onto a lightly floured surface. Divide the dough into 4 portions and set 1 portion aside. Divide each remaining portion into 8 pieces, making a total of 24. With floured hands, roll each piece into a ball, tucking in the edges. Put each ball into a greased muffin cup. Divide the reserved portion of dough into 24 pieces. Shape into balls. With a floured finger, make an indentation in each large ball. Press a small ball into each indentation.

Combine the egg white and 1 tablespoon water and brush lightly over the rolls. Cover and let rise until double in size, 45 to 55 minutes.

Preheat the oven to 375 degrees and bake for 15 minutes, brushing again with the egg-white wash after 7 minutes of baking time. Remove from the muffin tins when done and cool on wire racks.

When cooled completely, these may be frozen in a Ziploc bag and individually defrosted in the micro-wave for a spur-of-the-moment treat.

 Summer

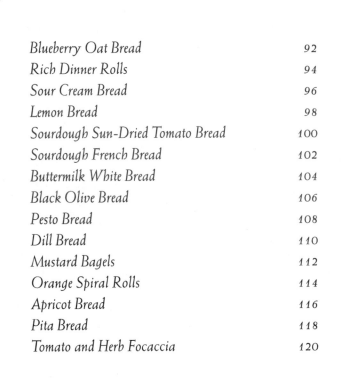

With summer comes the brightness of sky and sun; hot, sizzling pavements; ice-cold drinks; gardens abounding with tomatoes, zucchini, corn, and melons; vacations and weekend excursions; and soft, warm twilights.

Bread machines are perfect for this laid-back season. Measure the ingredients, select the cycle, and easily produce freshly baked bread, even on a sweltering summer's day. The sourdough recipes work very well during the summer because the Sourdough Starter (page 173) loves 80- to 90-degree days. Sourdough French Bread pairs nicely with a cold soup like gazpacho. Sourdough Sun-Dried Tomato Bread makes a lovely light supper paired with a spinach salad. The Orange Spiral Rolls are splendid served with melon for a quick, delicious breakfast. The sunny yellow Lemon Bread looks and tastes like a fresh summer's day—just slice some fruit, add an ice-cold drink, and you have a beautiful lunch.

For a cool summer meal, try the Pita Bread cut in half, split open, and filled with delicacies—sliced and sautéed vegetables, cooked meat covered with barbecue sauce, cold chicken salad, or an oriental fried-rice mixture. The Pita Bread recipe is a sturdy whole wheat variety with a nice depth of flavor.

The Tomato and Herb Focaccia is like a pizza, only smaller, and the dough itself is laced with the herbs and tomato. Toppings can be added before baking if desired. The focaccia is compact in size, so it travels well for vacations and day trips. With these easy and delicious bread recipes, you'll be sure to enjoy the long, warm days of summer.

Blueberry Oat Bread

A wholesome, nutritious loaf, with a crunchiness from the oats and a sweetness from the blueberries, this bread is moist, small-textured, and easy to slice. This is good bread to serve with a light crab-salad luncheon, or for breakfast instead of the usual muffins. It toasts into a wonderful snack, covered with butter, honey, or cream cheese.

1	cup water
2	tablespoons melted butter
3	tablespoons honey
1 ½	cups whole wheat flour
2	cups + 2 tablespoons unbleached flour
1	cup uncooked oats
1	teaspoon salt
¾	cup frozen blueberries
1	teaspoon dry yeast

Measure the water, melted butter, and honey into the bread
pan. Next add the whole wheat flour, unbleached flour, oats,
salt, and blueberries. Make a well in the dry ingredients
and measure in the yeast. Select the basic bread cycle for
a 2-pound loaf. Baking time will be about 50 minutes.

Rich Dinner Rolls

Wonderfully easy to work with, the dough is elastic and does not stick to your hands or utensils. The rolls bake up light, tender, and flaky, with a rich homemade flavor. Delicious with a salad lunch or for dinner. This recipe makes about 24 rolls.

1/2 cup milk

5 tablespoons melted butter, plus additional for brushing on rolls

6 tablespoons water

1 egg, lightly beaten

3 1/3 cups all-purpose flour

5 tablespoons sugar

1/2 teaspoon salt

1 teaspoon dry yeast

Measure the milk, melted butter, water, and egg into the bread pan. Add the flour, sugar, and salt. Make a well in the dry ingredients and measure in the yeast. Select the dough cycle on your bread machine, or if that is not available, select the basic bread cycle for a 1- to 1 1/2-pound loaf, and stop the machine after the dough has risen once.

Turn onto a lightly floured board and shape into cloverleaf rolls as follows: Break off 1-inch pieces of dough and roll into balls. Place 3 balls of dough in a greased muffin cup, so that they make one layer in the bottom of the cup and fill the cup about half full. Brush each with melted butter. Cover the rolls with a cloth and let rise in a warm place until double in size, about 30 to 45 minutes.

Preheat the oven to 400 degrees and bake for 12 to 15 minutes, or until golden brown. Turn out into a bread basket and serve or cool on a rack.

Butterfly rolls: Divide dough in half. Roll each half into a 15 × 7 inch rectangle; brush with melted butter. Roll up longest side tightly like a jelly roll. Cut the jelly roll crosswise into ten pieces (about 1 1/2 inches wide). Press down center of each piece with the back of a knife to form spiral butterfly wings. Put rolls on a buttered baking sheet, 1 inch apart. Preheat oven to 400 degrees and bake for 12 to 15 minutes.

Sour Cream Bread

This bread bakes into a light, airy loaf that is full of richness, moisture, and a hint of sour cream. It has a golden brown, crunchy crust and a coarse texture. It is especially good toasted with butter, jams, and honey spread on to fill the many holes with flavor. This bread is also delicious sliced thick and warmed for dinner.

3	tablespoons melted butter
$^3/_4$	cup water
$^3/_4$	cup sour cream, room temperature
$3\,^3/_4$	cups all-purpose flour
1	tablespoon sugar
1	teaspoon salt
$2\,^1/_4$	teaspoons (1 package) dry yeast

Measure the melted butter, water, and sour cream into the bread pan. Add the flour, sugar, and salt. Make a well in the dry ingredients and pour in the yeast. Select the basic bread cycle for a 1- to 1½-pound loaf. Baking time will be approximately 40 minutes.

Lemon Bread

Perfect for summer's outdoor breakfasts and luncheons, this beautiful pastel yellow bread goes especially well with seafood salads. It is a large, light, airy and even-textured loaf. The lemony flavor is delicate with the occasional zing of a crunchy lemon peel.

³/₄	cup milk
3	tablespoons melted butter
1	tablespoon lemon juice
2	eggs, lightly beaten
3	cups + 2 tablespoons all-purpose flour
3	tablespoons sugar
1	teaspoon salt
1	tablespoon grated lemon rind
2¹/₄	teaspoons (1 package) dry yeast

Measure the milk, butter, lemon juice, and eggs into the bread pan. Add the flour, sugar, salt, and lemon rind. Make a well in the dry ingredients and add the yeast. Select the basic bread cycle for a 1- to 1¹/₂-pound loaf. Baking time should be not longer than 40 minutes because the crust has a tendency to burn if over-baked.

Sourdough Sun-Dried Tomato Bread

The subtle blending of the sourdough and dried tomato make this bread unique and flavorful. The tomatoes also give it a gentle orange-red color with bright bits of red tomato flecked throughout. This is a soft, easy-to-slice loaf that's good with lunch or dinner, as sandwich bread, or as a side to pasta.

½ cup Sourdough Starter (see page 173),
     room temperature
1   cup water
2   teaspoons canola or olive oil
1   teaspoon honey
1½ cups whole wheat flour
2½ cups unbleached flour
1   teaspoon salt
⅓ cup oil-packed sun-dried tomatoes, drained
1   teaspoon dry yeast

Measure the Sourdough Starter, water, oil, and honey into the bread pan. Add the whole wheat flour, unbleached flour, salt, and sun-dried tomatoes. Make a well in the dry ingredients and measure in the yeast. Select the basic bread cycle for a 1- to 1½-pound loaf. Baking time will be about 40 minutes.

Variations to this bread can be made by adding ½ teaspoon of any type of dried herb (rosemary, basil, thyme, etc.) to the bread pan when measuring in the dry ingredients.

Sourdough
French Bread

Serve this sturdy loaf with Italian food, hot chili, soups, and salads. The crunchy crust covers a moist, tender, sourdough middle with a fine, even texture. The flavor is tangy and robust. A serrated knife slices this bread cleanly. It is wonderful warmed, thickly sliced, and spread with butter.

$^3/_4$ cup water
1   cup Sourdough Starter (see page 173),
     room temperature
3 $^1/_2$ cups all-purpose flour
2   teaspoons sugar
1   teaspoon salt
2 $^1/_4$ teaspoons (1 package) dry yeast

Measure the water and Sourdough Starter into the bread pan. Add the flour, sugar, and salt. Make a well in the dry ingredients and measure in the yeast. Select the French bread cycle on your bread machine. If your machine does not have this option, choose the basic bread cycle for a 2-pound loaf with a dark crust. Baking time will be about 65 minutes. Watch during the last five minutes of baking time and stop the baking cycle early if the crust is getting too dark.

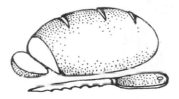

Buttermilk White Bread

The combination of the buttermilk and yeast creates a delicate texture, smooth, rich flavor, and wonderful moistness. This is a large loaf with a dark honey-colored crust. Good for toasting, snacks, and sandwiches, it stores well in the refrigerator or the freezer.

1	cup buttermilk
1/2	cup water
3	tablespoons melted butter
4	cups unbleached flour
1	tablespoon sugar
1	teaspoon salt
2 1/4	teaspoons (1 package) dry yeast

Measure the buttermilk, water, and melted butter into the bread pan. Add the unbleached flour, sugar, and salt. Make a well in the dry ingredients and measure in the yeast. Set the machine to the basic bread cycle for a 2-pound loaf. Baking time will be approximately 50 minutes.

Black Olive Bread

With an excellent Italian flavor from the olives
and herbs, this bread bakes to a crunchy crust
with a soft center. It has an even texture and is
great for lunches or with dinner.

3	tablespoons olive or canola oil
3/4	cup water
3	cups unbleached flour
1	(5 1/2-ounce) can black pitted sliced olives, drained to make 1 cup, coarsely chopped
1	teaspoon salt
1/2	teaspoon onion powder
1/2	teaspoon dried oregano flakes
1/2	teaspoon dried basil flakes
1	teaspoon dry yeast

Measure the oil and water into the bread pan. Add the flour, olives, salt, onion powder, oregano, and basil. Make a well in the dry ingredients and measure in the yeast. Select the basic bread cycle for a 1- to 1 1/2-pound loaf with a baking time of approximately 40 minutes.

Or, after the dough has risen once, take it out of the pan and divide in half. Flatten each half into a circle, gather the edges toward the center, and knead each piece of dough into a ball. Sprinkle a baking sheet with 1 tablespoon cornmeal, and set the dough on this. Cover with a cloth, put in a warm place, and let the dough rise until doubled in size. This will take about 1 hour. Adjust the oven rack to the lowest position. Preheat the oven to 400 degrees. Using a sharp razor or knife, make an X in the top of each ball. Bake until the loaves are golden brown, 25 to 30 minutes. Cool to room temperature before slicing.

Pesto Bread

The pesto adds a unique flavor and moistness to this zesty, aromatic bread. It bakes to a light golden crust with a mouthwatering fragrance. It is an excellent companion to soups, stews, salads, and Italian food and also can be a creative and nutritious snack.

$^1/_2$ cup basil pesto (homemade or store-bought)
1   cup water
2   tablespoons canola or olive oil
$3^3/_4$ cups unbleached flour
1   teaspoon salt
$2^1/_4$ teaspoons (1 package) dry yeast

Measure the pesto, water, and oil into the bread pan. Add the flour and salt. Make a well in the dry ingredients and add the yeast. Select the basic bread cycle for a 1- to $1^1/_2$-pound loaf. Baking time will be approximately 40 minutes.

Variations can easily be done with this bread just by changing the type of pesto used.

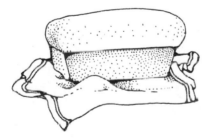

Dill Bread

The dill sends out a wonderful aroma as the bread is baking. This gently flavored bread bakes to a soft tender middle, with a nice golden crust. It slices well and toasts firmly and is a good companion at lunch or dinner. It's a unique bread that makes a fun change from the ordinary.

¹/₄	cup water
1	cup cottage cheese, room temperature
1	egg, lightly beaten
1 ¹/₂	tablespoons melted butter
2 ¹/₂	cups + 3 tablespoons all-purpose flour
2	tablespoons sugar
1	teaspoon dried dill weed
1	teaspoon salt
2 ¹/₄	teaspoons (1 package) dry yeast

Measure the water, cottage cheese, egg, and melted butter into the bread pan. Add the flour, sugar, dill weed, and salt. Make a well in the dry ingredients and measure in the yeast. Select the basic bread cycle for a 1- to 1¹/₂-pound loaf. Baking time will be about 40 minutes.

Mustard Bagels

The mustard brings a unique flavor to these bagels, which are crusty on the outside and nice and tender on the inside. These are great for sandwiches, toasted with cream cheese, or all by themselves, just warmed.

³/₄	cup + 1 tablespoon milk
¹/₄	cup melted butter
1	egg, lightly beaten
3	tablespoons spicy brown mustard
3 ³/₄	cups all-purpose flour
1	teaspoon salt
2 ¹/₄	teaspoons (1 package) dry yeast

Measure the milk, melted butter, lightly beaten egg, and mustard into the bread pan. Add the flour and salt. Make a well in the dry ingredients and measure in the yeast. Select the dough cycle. If your machine does not have this cycle, then choose the basic bread cycle and stop the machine after the dough has risen once.

Turn the dough out onto a lightly floured board. Divide the dough into 12 equal pieces. Roll each piece into a ball, poke a hole in the middle of the dough with your finger, and stretch the hole so that the dough looks like a doughnut. Place the bagels on a lightly greased cookie sheet, cover with a cloth, and allow to rise for 30 minutes.

In a large kettle, bring 2 quarts of lightly salted water to a boil. Drop 2 or 3 bagels into the water at a time and cook about 3 minutes on each side. Remove with a slotted utensil and place back on the cookie sheet.

When all 12 bagels have been boiled, preheat the oven to 375 degrees and bake for 23 to 25 minutes, or until lightly golden brown. Cool on wire racks. When completely cooled, these bagels may be frozen in a Ziploc freezer bag.

Variations can be made by changing the type of mustard used: hotter and spicier, or mild and sweet. To make the flavor stronger, an extra tablespoon of mustard can be added to the initial ingredients, taking care to add one more tablespoon flour, if necessary, for the correct consistency.

Orange Spiral Rolls

This easy-to-work-with dough bakes up delicate
and light. These rolls are not too sweet—an
outstanding orange flavor subtly blends with
the sugar. Excellent for breakfast or coffee, they
travel and store well. This recipe makes 24 rolls.

The Dough

²/₃ cup water
¹/₃ cup orange juice
¹/₄ cup melted butter
2 eggs, lightly beaten
4¹/₂ cups all-purpose flour
1 teaspoon salt
¹/₄ cup sugar
2¹/₄ teaspoons (1 package) dry yeast

Orange Filling

2 tablespoons melted butter, divided
¹/₄ cup sugar
1 orange rind, grated

Measure the water, orange juice, butter, and eggs into the bread pan. Add the flour, salt, and sugar. Make a well in the dry ingredients and add the yeast. Choose the dough cycle on your bread machine; or if your machine does not have this option, choose the basic bread cycle and stop the machine after the dough has risen once.

Turn the dough onto a lightly floured board and divide in half. Roll each half into a 12 × 8 inch rectangle. Brush on 1 tablespoon of the melted butter for the filling. Mix the sugar and the orange rind and sprinkle half of this mixture over the butter. Roll the dough up like a jelly roll. Cut into 12 even slices. Place the slices cut-side down in a greased or sprayed muffin tin. Repeat this process with the second portion of dough. Cover the tins with a cloth and allow the rolls to rise until double in size, about 30 minutes.

Preheat the oven to 375 degrees and bake for 15 minutes. When done baking, allow the rolls to cool 5 minutes in the muffin pans, then remove them to wire racks for complete cooling. These can then be frozen in Ziploc bags if they are to be stored for any length of time.

Variations: Lemon peel and lemon juice can be used instead of the orange; nuts and/or raisins can be added.

Apricot Bread

The cottage cheese in this loaf makes it moist and full of protein. The apricots add their subtle flavor, chewiness, and rich fiber. It is a delicious, even-textured bread for breakfast or tea, warmed or toasted, with butter, cream cheese, or honey. It freezes well.

1	cup water
1	cup cottage cheese, room temperature
2	tablespoons canola oil
2	tablespoons honey
3 ¾	cups whole wheat flour
¾	cup dried, chopped apricots
½	teaspoon salt
2 ¼	teaspoons (1 package) dry yeast

Measure the water, cottage cheese, oil, and honey into the bread pan. Add the flour, apricots, and salt. Make a well in the dry ingredients and measure in the yeast. Select the basic whole wheat bread cycle for a 1- to 1 ½-pound loaf. Baking time will be 40 to 45 minutes.

Pita Bread

A simple recipe that uses easy-to-work-with dough, this pita bread can be done quickly in the morning in time to have pita bread for lunch. As the pita breads cool, the pockets become more pronounced. This pita has a solid whole wheat flavor that enhances any sandwich for lunch or dinner. This recipes makes about 11 pitas depending on the actual size and thickness of the buns.

1 ²/₃ cups water
1   teaspoon honey
2   tablespoons canola oil
3 ²/₃ cups whole wheat flour
¹/₂   cup brown rice flour
2   tablespoons wheat germ
1   teaspoon salt
2 ¹/₄ teaspoons (1 package) dry yeast

Measure the water, honey, and oil into the bread pan. Next
add the whole wheat flour, brown rice flour, wheat germ, and
salt. Make a well in the dry ingredients and pour the yeast into
the well. Select the dough cycle, or if your machine does not
have this option, select the basic bread cycle for a 1- to 1¹/₂-
pound loaf and stop the machine after the dough has risen once.

On a floured board, roll the dough to ¹/₂-inch thick. Cut
the dough into circles about 4 inches in diameter, using a lid
or a regular bun cutter. Flour may need to be dusted on the
cutting utensil each time a circle is cut. Continue rolling and
cutting until all the dough has been cut. Place the circles on
an oiled cookie sheet.

For shiny tops, brush the circles with a beaten egg to which
¹/₄ teaspoon water has been added. Then sprinkle with sesame
seeds, poppy seeds, sunflower seeds, onion powder, herbs, or
any other flavoring that you choose. Cover and let rise for
an hour.

Preheat the oven to 500 degrees. Bake for 10 minutes or
until golden in color. Cool on a wire rack until there is no
warmth left and then store in a Ziploc bag.

Tomato and Herb Focaccia

This flatbread bakes to a chewy, herb-laced delight. It originated in Italy and is wonderful as a healthful snack, as the main dish for lunch, or as a side dish to dinner. It is best eaten warm right out of the oven because it tends to dry out and does not stay fresh much longer than a day.

THE DOUGH

1 1/4 cups water
3 3/4 cups unbleached flour
1 teaspoon salt
1/3 cup oil-packed sun-dried tomatoes, drained, patted dry, and cut in pieces
2 1/4 teaspoons (1 package) dry yeast

TOPPINGS

6 tablespoons olive oil and one or more of the following:
1/2 teaspoon dried oregano; 3/4 teaspoon dried summer savory; 1/2 teaspoon ground black pepper; 1/2 teaspoon ground rosemary; a sprinkling of minced garlic, chopped onion, olives, crushed red peppers, parmesan cheese, etc.

Measure the water into the bread pan. Add the flour, salt, and sun-dried tomatoes. Make a well in the dry ingredients and measure in the yeast. Select the dough cycle, or if your machine does not have this option, select the basic bread cycle, and stop the machine after the dough has risen once.

Coat a 15 × 10 inch jelly-roll pan, or cookie sheet, with 3 tablespoons of the oil. Remove the dough from the bread pan, place on a lightly floured board, and roll the dough into a rectangle large enough to fill the jelly-roll pan. Drizzle the top with 1 tablespoon of the oil. Cover and let rise for 30 minutes in a warm place.

Next dimple the top of the dough by poking 1/2-inch holes in the top with oiled fingertips. These holes make little caves for the spices, herbs, and toppings to nestle in. Cover with a cloth and let rise another 1 1/2 hours.

Sprinkle the oregano, savory, and pepper, and any other choice of toppings over the dough; drizzle with the remaining 2 tablespoons of oil.

Adjust the oven rack to the lowest position and preheat the oven to 425 degrees. Bake 18 to 20 minutes, spraying water into the oven with a water sprayer a couple of times the first 5 to 10 minutes. Bake until the bottom of the crust is lightly colored. Cut the focaccia into 2-inch squares and serve warm.

Autumn

The joys of Thanksgiving and family encompass this mellow season with the soft browns and golden yellows of dried leaves and grasses and the deep reds and oranges of autumn foliage. Outside fires smell of burning leaves; days are shorter with cooler nights. Autumn is the beginning of sweatshirts and sweaters, crisp, juicy, red apples, and thick soups filled with just-harvested root vegetables.

Sturdy, hearty-flavored breads are perfect at this time of year. Seeded Rye Bread, Mustard Rye Bread and Sourdough Pumpernickel Bread epitomize the health-sustaining, rib-sticking goodness of autumn foods. Pumpkin Bread has a spice-laden flavor and aroma that is Thanksgiving, combined with the lightness of a yeast bread—it's good with any meal. As the weather cools, robust whole wheat breads fuel our bodies. Whole-Wheat Sesame Bread, Honey Oatmeal Wheat Bread, Sourdough Whole Wheat English Muffins, and Beer Wheat Bread are a just few of the wheat recipes included in this autumn selection.

For Monday Night Football fans, the Pizza, Soft Bread-sticks, and Cheddar-Cumin Rolls pair with favorite snacks to become part of the tradition. For Thanksgiving, serve tender Sweet Potato Buns. It's a rich season full of the hearty goodness so evident in these recipes.

Honey Oatmeal Wheat Bread

As this bread bakes, the scent of warm cinnamon and oatmeal permeates the air. The flavor is just as good as it smells. It bakes to a light golden brown loaf, and is excellent toasted or warmed for breakfast, along with some fruit. The texture is coarse, so thoroughly cool before slicing.

1 ½   cups water
2   tablespoons melted butter
3   tablespoons honey
2   cups unbleached flour
1 ½   cups whole wheat flour
1   cup uncooked rolled oats
1   teaspoon salt
½   teaspoon ground cinnamon
2 ¼   teaspoons (1 package) dry yeast

Measure the water, melted butter, and honey into the bread pan. Add the unbleached flour, the whole wheat flour, and the oatmeal. Add the salt and cinnamon. Make a well in the dry ingredients and pour in the yeast. Select the basic bread cycle for a 2-pound loaf. The baking time will be about 50 minutes.

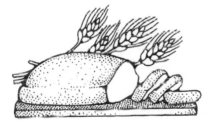

Pumpkin Bread

The pumpkin turns this bread a gorgeous golden yellow and also makes it very moist. It is different than a pumpkin quick bread because the yeast creates an airiness to the texture. The subtle flavor of pumpkin is enhanced by the rich spices. Serve it thickly sliced with a Halloween soup, as part of a leftover turkey and cranberry sandwich, or as a colorful addition to a holiday buffet.

¹/₂	cup milk
2	tablespoons melted butter
¹/₂	cup puréed pumpkin (homemade or canned)
2	tablespoons water
3	cups + 2 tablespoons all-purpose flour
2	tablespoons chopped walnuts, pecans, or almonds
3	tablespoons sugar
¹/₂	teaspoon salt
¹/₂	teaspoon cinnamon
¹/₈	teaspoon cloves
¹/₄	teaspoon nutmeg
2¹/₄	teaspoons (1 package) dry yeast

Measure the milk, melted butter, pumpkin, and water into the bread pan. Add the flour, nuts, sugar, salt, cinnamon, cloves, and nutmeg. Make a well in the dry ingredients and add the yeast. Select the basic bread cycle for a 1- to 1¹/₂-pound loaf of bread. Baking time will be about 40 minutes.

Brown Rice Bread

A moist loaf with a coarse texture, this bread has an old-fashioned look and smell. The flavor is nutty and the texture is intermittently crunchy from the brown rice. It is a bread that can be used for sandwiches and toast, or served with dinner. It keeps well in the refrigerator or freezer because of the moistness of the rice.

THE RICE	THE DOUGH

THE RICE
1 1/2 cups water
1/2 cup raw brown rice

THE DOUGH
1 cup water
4 cups unbleached flour
1 1/2 teaspoons brown sugar
1 teaspoon salt
1 teaspoon dry yeast

In a saucepan bring the 1 1/2 cups water to a boil. Add the 1/2 cup brown rice, turn the heat down to low, cover, and simmer until the rice is done, about 50 minutes. Let the rice cool as you work with the rest of the ingredients.

Measure the 1 cup water into the bread pan. Add 3 2/3 cups of the flour, reserving about 1/3 cup. In the saucepan, mix the 1/3 cup flour and the cooked rice, so that the rice grains are coated. Then pour the rice and flour mixture into the bread pan. Add the sugar and salt. Make a well in the dry ingredients and measure in the yeast. Choose the basic bread cycle for a 2-pound loaf. Baking time will be approximately 50 minutes.

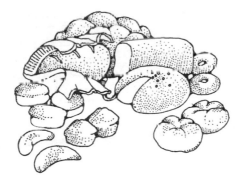

Autumn

Sourdough Pumpernickel Bread

A beautiful dark brown bread with a hearty, deep pumpernickel flavor that is mingled with the sourdough tang. It is very moist and has an even texture that is perfect for slicing. This makes wonderful deli sandwiches. This bread is also delicious toasted and spread liberally with cream cheese.

$^1/_2$	cup Sourdough Starter (see page 173), room temperature
$^3/_4$	cup milk
1	tablespoon molasses
2	tablespoons canola oil
1 $^1/_4$	cups unbleached flour
$^3/_4$	cup rye flour
1	cup whole wheat flour
2	tablespoons cocoa
1	tablespoon instant coffee
$^1/_2$	teaspoon salt
1	teaspoon dry yeast

Measure the Sourdough Starter, milk, molasses, and oil into the bread pan. Add the unbleached flour, rye flour, whole wheat flour, cocoa, instant coffee, and salt. Make a well in the dry ingredients and add the yeast. Select the basic bread cycle for a 1- to 1 $^1/_2$-pound loaf. Baking time will be about 40 minutes.

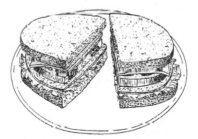

Raisin and Nut Bread

*Excellent for breakfast, try serving this small,
dense loaf with butter, honey, and/or cream cheese.
It freezes well.*

¹/₄　cup raisins
¹/₄　cup water
3　　tablespoons melted butter
³/₄　cup milk
1　　tablespoon honey
3　　cups unbleached flour
1　　teaspoon salt
¹/₄　cup chopped walnuts (or pecans, unsalted peanuts,
　　filberts, or almonds)
1　　teaspoon yeast

Soak the raisins in a little warm water for an hour or so, drain them, and then prepare the dough.

Measure the water, butter, milk, and honey into the bread pan. Add the flour, salt, raisins, and nuts. (If your machine has a cycle for adding the fruit and nuts later, then follow those directions.) Make a well in the dry ingredients and add the yeast. Select the basic bread cycle for a 1- to 1 ¹/₂-pound loaf. The baking time will be about 40 minutes.

Irish Oatmeal Bread

An old-fashioned bread—coarse-textured and heartily flavorful with wheat and oats—this is wonderful with soups and stews. The currants add a light sweetness. Eating this bread in thick slices spread with butter brings to mind days gone by.

1   cup water
3   tablespoons honey
$^1/_4$ cup canola oil
1   egg, beaten
3 $^1/_2$ cups whole wheat flour
1   cup rolled oats
2   tablespoons nonfat dry milk
$^1/_2$ teaspoon salt
$^1/_2$ cup currants
2 $^1/_4$ teaspoons (1 package) dry yeast

Measure the water, honey, and oil into the bread pan, and add the egg. Next measure in the whole wheat flour, rolled oats, dry milk, salt, and currants. Make a well in the dry ingredients and add the yeast. Select the basic bread cycle for a 1- to 1$^1/_2$-pound loaf. The baking time will be about 40 minutes.

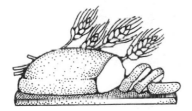

Sourdough Whole Wheat English Muffins

These English muffins can be served fresh off the griddle; or allow them to cool, then split and toast them. They have a dense texture and are nice and moist and full of tangy sourdough and whole wheat flavor. This recipe makes about 18 muffins.

1 1/4 cups water
1/2 cup Sourdough Starter (see page 173),
     room temperature
2 teaspoons honey
2 tablespoons canola oil
4 1/2 cups whole wheat flour
1/2 cup nonfat dry milk
1 teaspoon salt
1 teaspoon dry yeast

Measure the water, Sourdough Starter, honey, and oil into the bread pan. Add the whole wheat flour, nonfat dry milk, and salt. Make a well in the dry ingredients and measure in the yeast. Select the dough cycle. If your machine does not have this option, then choose the basic whole wheat bread cycle and stop the machine after the dough has risen once.

Turn the dough out onto a floured board. Roll the dough out to a thickness of about 3/8 inch. Cut the dough with a round cutter that is 2 1/2 to 3 inches in diameter. Place the muffins on a lightly greased or sprayed cookie sheet. Cover with a cloth and let them rise for about 1 hour.

Heat an iron skillet or griddle on medium heat. Lightly oil or spray the griddle. Bake the muffins for about 7 minutes on each side, making sure that the middle of the muffin is fully cooked. The crust bakes up nice and golden brown.

Beer Wheat Bread

*Evenly textured with a hearty, deep wheat flavor,
this bread has a dark brown crust, and enough
moistness for easy slicing. It is excellent toasted
with jam or honey, sturdy enough for sandwiches,
and a good complement to an autumn meal.*

6 ounces (^{3}/$_4$ cup) stout beer
3 tablespoons melted butter
^{1}/$_4$ cup milk
3 tablespoons honey
3 cups whole wheat flour
^{1}/$_2$ cup wheat germ
^{1}/$_2$ teaspoon salt
2^1/$_4$ teaspoons (1 package) dry yeast

Measure the beer, melted butter, milk, and honey into the bread pan. Add the flour, wheat germ, and salt. Make a well in the dry ingredients and measure in the yeast. Select the basic whole wheat cycle for a 1- to 1^1/$_2$-pound loaf of bread. Baking time will be about 45 minutes.

Seeded Oat-Flour Bread

The oat flour creates a very moist, dense texture in this bread. It has a smooth wheat flavor, enhanced by the crunchiness of the sunflower seeds. This bread can be sliced thick for hearty sandwiches, or toasted for a delicious quick breakfast.

1 1/4 cups water
1/4   cup honey
2   tablespoons melted butter
1   egg, lightly beaten
1 1/2 cups oat flour
3   cups whole wheat flour
2   tablespoons sunflower seeds
1   teaspoon salt
2 1/4 teaspoons (1 package) dry yeast

Measure the water, honey, butter, and egg into the bread pan. Add the oat flour, whole wheat flour, sunflower seeds, and salt. Make a well in the dry ingredients and measure in the yeast. Select the basic whole wheat bread cycle for a 2-pound loaf. Baking time will be about 55 minutes.

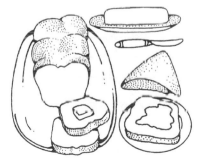

Parmesan-Oregano Bread

As this bread bakes, it creates a savory, delicious smell that is all Italian. The Parmesan cheese makes the loaf extra moist and adds to the flavor. This bread bakes to a large loaf with a golden brown crust and an even texture. It slices easily when cooled, and can be frozen successfully. It is very good warmed for dinner or sliced thick for a sandwich.

1 ½ cups water
2   tablespoons melted butter
4 ½ cups all-purpose flour
½   cup grated Parmesan cheese
2   shakes of garlic powder
1 ½ teaspoons dried oregano flakes
2   tablespoons sugar
1   teaspoon salt
2 ¼ teaspoons (1 package) dry yeast

Pour the water and melted butter into the bread pan. Add the flour, Parmesan cheese, garlic powder, oregano, sugar, and salt. Make a well in the dry ingredients and pour in the yeast. Select the basic bread cycle for a 2-pound loaf. The baking time should be about 50 minutes.

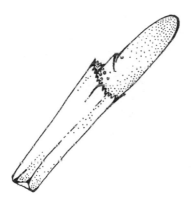

Mustard Rye Bread

A small loaf with nice even texture, this bread has a wonderfully mellow mustard flavor and makes an outstanding sandwich. The rye flour adds a little kick and crunchiness to the bread. It's perfect for snacks with cream cheese and chives. Toasted, it makes a delicious patty melt with hamburger, onions, and cheese. This loaf keeps well.

1	cup water
2	tablespoons canola oil
2	tablespoons spicy brown mustard
2	cups all-purpose flour
1 1/4	cups rye flour
1	tablespoon brown sugar
1	teaspoon salt
2 1/4	teaspoons (1 package) dry yeast

Measure the water, oil, and mustard into the bread pan. Add the all-purpose flour, rye flour, brown sugar, and salt. Make a well in the dry ingredients and measure in the yeast. Select the basic bread cycle for a 1- to 1 1/2-pound loaf. The baking time will be about 40 minutes.

Variations can be created by using different flavors of mustard, from the heat of mustard-horseradish to the mildness of yellow mustard. Have fun!

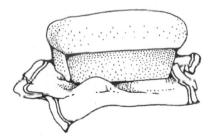

Applesauce–Carrot Bread

*Try serving this wonderfully moist, flavorful
bread warm with butter, honey, cream cheese, or
apple butter. The texture is even, making the loaf
easy to slice, and it has just a touch of sweetness
and spice. It makes a delicious, healthful snack.
Or try it as a breakfast bread with hot cereal.*

1	cup milk
1/2	cup applesauce
1	tablespoon canola oil
2	cups whole wheat flour
2	cups unbleached flour
1/4	cup sugar
1	teaspoon salt
1	teaspoon cinnamon
1/2	cup grated carrot
2 1/4	teaspoons (1 package) dry yeast

Measure the milk, applesauce, and oil into the bread pan. Add the whole wheat flour, unbleached flour, sugar, salt, cinnamon, and grated carrot. Make a well in the dry ingredients and measure in the yeast. Select the basic whole wheat bread cycle for a 2-pound loaf. Baking time will be about 50 minutes.

Pizza

This is a good sturdy pizza dough with a subtle flavor that goes well with a wide range of toppings. Try topping the basic tomato sauce and cheese with one or more of the following: Canadian bacon, sausage, sliced onions, sliced olives, chopped green peppers, sliced artichoke hearts, sliced mushrooms, Parmesan cheese, tomatoes . . . whatever suits your taste buds.

The Dough

1 cup water
3 1/2 cups unbleached flour
1 teaspoon sugar
1 teaspoon salt
2 1/4 teaspoons (1 package) dry yeast

Basic Topping

1 cup pizza sauce (homemade or store-bought)
12 ounces shredded mozzarella cheese

Measure the water into the bread pan. Add the flour, sugar, and salt. Make a well in the dry ingredients and measure in the yeast. Select the dough cycle. If your machine does not have this cycle, select the basic bread cycle and stop the machine after the dough has risen once.

Sprinkle cornmeal on the bottom of a cookie sheet. Spread the dough to evenly cover the pan, making a ridge around the edges. Cover the dough with the sauce and cheese, and your choice of toppings.

Preheat the oven to 375 degrees and bake for 20 minutes, or until the crust is golden brown. Cut into individual pieces.

Peppery Parmesan Bread

A Parmesan cheese flavor laced with pepper pervades this light, moist, even-textured bread. It is super as a sandwich bread with lots of deli meats and cheeses in it and as an accompaniment to thick minestrone soup and other hearty soups and stews.

1 ¹/₃   cups water
2   tablespoons canola oil
4   cups unbleached flour
¹/₂   teaspoon salt
¹/₂   teaspoon black pepper
1   teaspoon sugar
¹/₂   cup finely grated Parmesan cheese
2 ¹/₄   teaspoons (1 package) dry yeast

Measure the water and oil into the bread pan. Add the unbleached flour, salt, black pepper, sugar, and Parmesan cheese.
Make a well in the dry ingredients and add the yeast. Select
the basic bread cycle for a 2-pound loaf. Baking time will be
about 50 minutes.

Variations can include 1 teaspoon of any type of dried
herb, such as basil, oregano, or thyme.

Sweet Potato Buns

Serve this light fluffy roll with dinner on a crisp Autumn evening. They're a beautiful sweet potato color and their flavor is subtle, unique, and old-fashioned. This recipe makes about 18 rolls.

1	medium sweet potato
1/3	cup sweet potato cooking water, cooled (see below)
3	tablespoons honey
1	tablespoon melted butter
3/4	cup milk
4	cups unbleached flour
1	teaspoon salt
2 1/4	teaspoons (1 package) dry yeast

Peel and cut the sweet potato in small pieces. Cover with water and cook until tender (about 20 minutes). Drain, reserving 1/3 cup of the cooking water, and mash the sweet potato. Let the water and the mashed potato cool.

Measure the sweet potato and water, the honey, butter, and milk into the bread pan. Add the flour and salt. Make a well in the dry ingredients and measure in the yeast. Select the dough cycle. If your machine does not have this cycle, select the basic bread cycle and stop the machine after the dough has risen once.

Take the dough out of the bread pan, put onto a floured board and knead 1 to 2 minutes. (This dough is very moist and soft to work. Flour on the board and on your hands is necessary for easy handling.) Pinch off pieces of the dough about the size of golf balls and place each one in a section of a greased muffin tin. Cover and let rise until doubled in size (about 1 hour).

Preheat the oven to 425 degrees and bake for 15 minutes. Allow the rolls to cool 5 minutes in the muffin tins and then remove them to a wire rack for thorough cooling. These can be frozen or refrigerated when completely cooled.

Whole Wheat Sesame Bread

This recipe bakes into a small, sturdy loaf with a dense, crunchy texture and a good whole wheat flavor. It makes hearty sandwiches and goes well with soups and stews.

1	tablespoon honey
1	cup water
1	tablespoon molasses
1	tablespoon canola oil
1 3/4	cups whole wheat flour
1 1/4	cups all-purpose flour
1/4	cup wheat germ
1	teaspoon salt
2	tablespoons sesame seeds
1	package dry yeast

Measure the honey, water, molasses, and oil into the bread pan. Add both flours, the wheat germ, salt, and sesame seeds. Make a well in the dry ingredients and measure in the yeast. Select the basic whole wheat bread cycle for a 1- to 1 1/2-pound loaf, with a baking time of about 45 minutes.

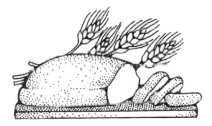

Molasses Bread

The finished loaf is a beautiful tan, moist, fine-textured, and packed with the flavor of molasses. As the bread bakes, its aroma entices, and it is hard to wait until the bread is done and cooled. Delicious toasted with butter and honey, it has a rich taste that is perfect for breakfast.

$^3/_4$ cup water
$^1/_2$ cup milk
2   tablespoons canola oil
3   tablespoons molasses
$4^1/_2$ cups unbleached flour
1   teaspoon salt
$2^1/_4$ teaspoons (1 package) dry yeast

Measure the water, milk, oil, and molasses into the bread pan. Add the flour and salt. Make a well in the flour and measure in the yeast. Select the basic bread cycle for a 2-pound loaf. Baking time will be approximately 50 minutes.

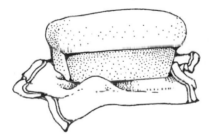

Cheddar-Cumin Rolls

This easy-to-handle dough bakes into light flavorful rolls with the moistness of cheese and the spiciness of cumin. Depending on the strength of cheddar used, the cheese flavor can be strong or just a mild hint. Baking the rolls on cornmeal gives the rolls a good crunchy crust.

These rolls are great with Tex-Mex or Mexican foods, and they freeze well. This recipe makes 12 rolls.

1 1/4   cups water
3 1/4   cups + 1 tablespoon unbleached flour
1   teaspoon sugar
1   teaspoon salt
1   teaspoon ground cumin
1   cup grated cheddar cheese, chilled
1   teaspoon dry yeast

Pour the water into the baking pan. Add the flour, sugar, salt, cumin, and cheese. Make a well in the dry ingredients and add the yeast. Select the dough cycle, or if your machine does not have this option, select the basic bread cycle and remove the dough after it has risen once.

Turn the dough out on a lightly floured surface, roll it into a ball, and cut it in half. Cut each half into six equal pieces. To shape each roll, take a piece, flatten it, and fold the corners inward while turning the dough clockwise. This gathers the edges toward the center; now pinch these edges together to form a tight ball of dough.

Sprinkle a baking sheet with a small dusting of cornmeal. Put the dough balls, pinched-sides down, at least 2 inches apart on the baking sheet. Cover with a lightweight cloth. Let rise until tripled in size, 1 1/2 to 2 hours

Adjust the oven rack to the lowest position. Preheat the oven to 450 degrees. Put the rolls in the oven and immediately spray them with cold water. Bake for 12 to 15 minutes or until the tops are golden. Cool before serving.

Sourdough Bread

The sourdough gives a light, airy texture to this bread, with the inherent sourdough flavor and moistness. This loaf needs to cool completely before being sliced. It is good toasted with butter and spread with jam, cream cheese, or as a broiled open-faced sandwich. It is also excellent with dinner, warmed and buttered, or broiled with garlic butter and/or Parmesan cheese.

$^1/_2$ cup + 1 tablespoon water
1   cup Sourdough Starter (see page 173),
       room temperature
1   tablespoon melted butter, cooled
3 $^1/_4$ cups all-purpose flour
1   teaspoon salt
1   tablespoon sugar
1   teaspoon dry yeast

Measure the water, Sourdough Starter, and melted butter into the bread pan. Add the flour, salt, and sugar. Make a well in the dry ingredients and add the yeast. Select the basic bread cycle for a 1- to 1$^1/_2$-pound loaf. Baking time will be approximately 40 minutes.

Seeded Rye Bread

A crunchy bread loaded with different flavors from the different seeds, this loaf bakes up light, airy, and moist, with the rye flavor bonding the variety of seeds together. It toasts well. Sliced thick, this bread creates lunch when topped with mustard, pastrami, onion slices, and cheese. Or try a hot roast beef and gravy sandwich for a quick tasty dish.

1	(12-ounce) can beer, room temperature
1	cup rye flour
3	cups + 2 tablespoons unbleached flour
1	teaspoon salt
2	tablespoons sugar
1	ounce Swiss or Gruyere cheese, shredded and chilled (about $^1/_4$ cup)
2	teaspoons sesame seeds
1	teaspoon caraway seeds
1	teaspoon poppy seeds
$2^1/_4$	teaspoons (1 package) dry yeast

Pour the beer into the bread pan. Next measure in the rye flour, unbleached flour, salt, sugar, cheese, sesame seeds, caraway seeds, and poppy seeds. Make a well in the dry ingredients and pour in the yeast. Choose the basic bread cycle for a 1- to 1$^1/_2$-pound loaf. Baking time will be about 40 minutes.

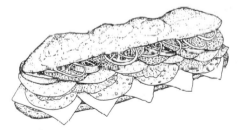

Soft Breadsticks

This dough is soft and a little sticky to work with. Keep your hands well dusted with flour as you're forming the dough into the bread sticks. The outside crust bakes up nice and crunchy; the inside is soft with good homemade flavor.

The Dough

1 1/2 cups water
1/4 cup olive or canola oil
3 3/4 cups all-purpose flour
1 tablespoon sugar
1 teaspoon salt
2 1/4 teaspoons (1 package) dry yeast

Topping

1 to 2 tablespoons sesame or poppy seeds
1 egg white beaten with 1 tablespoon water or
1 tablespoon melted butter
Garlic or onion powder

Measure the water and oil into the bread pan. Add the flour, sugar, and salt. Make a well in the dry ingredients and pour in the yeast. Select the dough cycle, or if your machine does not have this cycle, select the basic bread cycle and let the dough rise once; then stop the machine.

Turn the dough out onto a floured board. Let it rest for 3 minutes, then shape it into the bread sticks as follows: With a very sharp knife, cut the dough into 20 equal pieces. Using the palms of your hands roll out each piece to about 12-inches long on the floured board. Oil or butter baking sheets, sprinkling sesame or poppy seeds on top. Lay each bread stick down on the cookie sheet leaving about 1 inch between each.

To make twisted bread sticks, roll out to 12-inch sticks and then using two hands, pick up the rolls and twist, turning clockwise with one hand and counterclockwise with the other.

Let the formed breadsticks sit for 20 minutes, covered. Then brush each stick with the egg white and water mixture, or the melted butter. Sprinkle sesame seeds, poppy seeds, garlic powder, or onion powder over the breadsticks.

Preheat the oven to 350 degrees and bake for 30 minutes. They should be nicely browned and very crisp.

Store in an airtight container and they will stay crisp for several days.

Variations can include dried red pepper, Parmesan cheese, or Italian seasoning sprinkled on the breadsticks before baking.

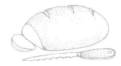 # Creating Sourdough

Sourdough starter is full of living organisms. You may find the bacteria that produce the sour smell and flavor to be a bit finicky at first. They need particular temperatures, food, and time to work their best magic in a bread.

Historically, sourdough starter was made by capturing bacteria in the air and allowing them to change the consistency of milk and flour. Their activity produced the necessary rising qualities that made a great loaf of bread. Once the starter was working well, it was fed and nurtured for the next bread-baking session. The starter was easy to pack, and miners, adventurers, and pioneers took it with them in their travels.

The following Sourdough Starter recipe is not made with wild bacteria but with the bacteria from yogurt. The bacteria in yogurt are consistent in behavior and produce a nice moist loaf with a full sourdough flavor. When the yogurt is added to the warm milk, it provides an environment in which the bacteria can grow; the flour provides the food.

There are two items that make this starter most successful when you begin. The first is that the yogurt and milk are fresh. This just means that they haven't been sitting in the refrigerator for days, becoming old and sluggish instead of healthy and productive. The second key to success is the temperature at which the Sourdough Starter is incubated. Just like a baby chick, the sourdough needs to be kept at a constant temperature between 80 to 90 degrees. This can be done by keeping the container near a continuously warm fire, on the top of a refrigerator, or on the counter during the warm summer months when the weather does not cool down. The temperature affects the starter. If it's too warm, the bacteria will die; if it's too cold, the starter will develop mold. In either case, it's time to begin all over again.

The exciting part about sourdough is that even if you have to begin again with a new starter, it is neither difficult nor expensive. It may take one or two tries to get your sourdough starter growing and healthy but it is so little work, after which very little attention is needed. The starter can be used extensively in breads, cakes, pancakes, biscuits, and rolls. It can also be shared with a friend or family member. Give that special someone a cup of starter in a unique but workable container, with recipes attached.

Enjoy the challenge, creativity, and delicious flavor of sourdough.

Sourdough Starter

This recipe makes about 1 1/3 cups of starter.

1   cup skim or lowfat milk
3   tablespoons plain yogurt
1   cup all-purpose flour

In a 1 quart pan over medium heat, heat the milk to 90 to
100 degrees. Remove from heat and stir in the yogurt. Pour
into a warm 3- to 6-cup glass, ceramic, plastic, or stainless steel
container with a tight lid. Let this stand in a warm place (80
to 90 degrees) until the mixture is the consistency of yogurt, a
curd has formed, and/or the mixture doesn't flow readily when
the container is tilted. This takes about 18 to 24 hours. If some
clear liquid has risen to the top of the mixture during this time,
stir it back in. If the liquid has turned a light pink, discard the
batch and start again.

Once the curd has formed, stir in the flour until smooth.
Cover tightly and let stand in a warm place until the mixture
is full of bubbles and has a good sour smell (about 2 days). If a
pink liquid forms, discard, and start the process again.

To store, keep it covered and refrigerate.

To feed the starter, first bring it to room temperature
by taking it out of the refrigerator for a couple of hours or
overnight. Add warm skim or lowfat milk and flour to the
starter in quantities equal to what you'll be using in the

recipe—that is, if you need 1 cup of starter, then add 1 cup of flour and 1 cup of warmed milk. Stir well and cover tightly. Let stand in a warm place until bubbly and sour-smelling and a clear liquid has formed on top (about 12 to 24 hours). Use or cover and chill. Stir before using.

To increase your starter supply, you can add up to 10 cups each of milk and flour to 1 cup of starter. This mixture may need to stand up to 2 days before the clear liquid forms on top.

Index